We were there

THE 1980s

Rosemary Rees

Heinemann

Heinemann Library,
an imprint of Heinemann Publishers (Oxford) Ltd,
Halley Court, Jordan Hill, Oxford, OX2 8EJ

OXFORD LONDON EDINBURGH
MADRID PARIS ATHENS BOLOGNA
MELBOURNE SYDNEY AUCKLAND
SINGAPORE TOKYO IBADAN
NAIROBI GABORONE HARARE
PORTSMOUTH NH (USA)

First published 1993
93 94 95 96 10 9 8 7 6 5 4 3 2 1

British Library Cataloguing in Publication Data
is available on request from the British Library.

ISBN 0 431 07326 0

Designed by Philip Parkhouse
Printed and bound in China

Acknowledgements
The author and publisher would like to thank the following
for permission to reproduce photographs:
Collections/David Bowie: p. 15
Collections/Brian Shuel: p. 14
Collections/Anthea Sieveking: p. 11
Edifice/Lewis: p. 27
Eye Ubiquitous/Paul Prestidge: p. 22
Eye Ubiquitous/Ben Spencer: p. 24
Impact/Peter Arkell: p.10, /Lionel Derimais: p. 7, /John Evens: p. 20,
Jeremy Nicholl: p. 30, /Caroline Penn: p. 23, /Geray Sweeney: p. 17
National Trust Photographic Library: p. 26
Philip Parkhouse: p. 21, /Rex Features: pp. 4, 28
Sally and Richard Greenhill: pp. 5, 6, 8, 9, 13, 19, 25
Science Photo Library/Martin Dohrn: p. 18
Science Photo Library/John Heseltine: p. 16

Cover photograph: Rex Features

The author and publisher would like to thank all of the people who
contributed memories for this book.

Note to the reader
In this book there are some words in the text which
are printed in **bold type**. This shows that the words
are listed in the glossary on page 31. The glossary gives
a brief explanation of words that may be new to you.

Contents

Home 1

In the 1980s more people started buying their own homes. A lot of new houses had to be built. They were built closer together so that the builders could make more money.

Margaret Hudson moved into a new house in the 1980s.

Our old house had been built about a hundred years ago. It had needed lots of mending. The roof had patches where there were new tiles, the bricks of the outside walls were breaking up, and the **guttering** was leaking. The garden was big, and we never really had the time to keep it tidy, or grow vegetables in it. The bathroom had an old metal bath in it. The new house was amazing. Everything was new.

The bricks were all new, the roof had the same tiles all over, the walls inside were really smooth. The kitchen had everything built into it, even the oven and the fridge. It was all so clean, and the loft smelt of sawdust, and there wasn't any dust. It took days and days for me to get used to how clean and new everything was. I was scared to use anything, or get the bath or the cooker dirty by using them! The back garden was smaller, just some grass and some paving stones.

Margaret Hudson was worried about getting the kitchen of her new house dirty.

I was quite scared of our kitchen in the new house, because it was so new. It was much smaller than our old kitchen. It was quite difficult for more than two people to be in it at the same time. The washing machine had a room of its own, called a **utility room**. You didn't have to spend a lot of time walking from one place to another when cooking, like you did in our old house. It had quite a lot of space to put things, even though it was small. But it had problems too. The fridge was built under the worksurface, and so it was quite small. Getting everything you needed into it was a problem. Also all of the cooking **gadgets** were electric. The oven, the microwave, the fridge, everything. This meant that when there was a **power cut** and the electricity went off you just couldn't cook anything. Our old house had a gas stove.

A fitted kitchen, with everything built into it. It had a cooker, a microwave and a dishwasher, and one of the bottom cupboard doors could be for a fridge.

Home 2

In the 1980s, more people had machines like record and CD players, TVs and videos. All these got a lot cheaper. If they could only afford one thing it would usually be a TV.

Fiona Grey remembers how her boys were more at home with the new equipment than she was.

We had had a TV for quite a while, but then my husband and the boys started saying that they really wanted a video too. They went on a lot about being able to tape educational programmes that they would otherwise miss, but I think they were really thinking about hiring films! We got one in the end, and the boys learnt how to set it far quicker than I did. It wasn't really difficult, but I don't like machinery, I always expect it to go wrong. My oldest son, Thomas, has always been really good at mechanical things. He understood the video in about five minutes. The same thing happened with computers, when they came into our home. The boys could understand them really quickly. I was much less keen to use them. I think it helped that the boys were taught about computers at school. I am glad that we got the video, though.

Judith Maguire didn't always enjoy supermarket shopping.

I found the big supermarkets quite frightening sometimes. They were very big. Sometimes I panicked, not every time I went, but sometimes. When this happened I had to leave my trolley and go out into the car park, and just wait out there for a bit. I liked to shop on my own with a list to follow rather than shopping with someone who wanted to wander around looking at everything.

Jane Gross found other problems with big supermarkets.

It was very difficult to go into the supermarket and just buy what you needed. There was so much to choose from, so many things that you could have. So you would go in to buy just a few things, but you would fill a trolley with things that were on special offer. You ended up spending more money than you really needed to. I used to have to really work hard to make myself buy just the things we needed.

In the 1980s, supermarkets started selling fresh food, like fish, meat and fruit and vegetables. People could buy everything they needed at one shop.

Home 3

The Metro Centre, Gateshead, Newcastle-on-Tyne, was one of the first big shopping complexes. These had lots of different shops under one roof, and places to eat as well.

Jane Gross went to visit the Metro Centre with her family and some friends.

I had heard about the Metro Centre, and when we went to stay with friends in Newcastle they took us there. It was huge. There were lots of different shops. You could buy anything there, from clothes to garden tools. These shops were on more than one level, and there were lifts and escalators to go up and down. I can't remember if there were two or three levels, now.

There were plants, and places to sit on benches, even fountains, all indoors. There were lots of places to eat. You could get ice cream, pizza, burgers, cakes and buns to eat on the benches, or you could go into cafés to sit down and eat. There was even a huge play area, with a **ball pit** and lots of slides and ropes and **scramble nets**. These were joined up with lots of walkways. There were even computer game arcades. We spent all day there. I think people went there for a day out.

Barbecues in the garden became very popular in the 1980s, even though the weather in Britain isn't very good for outdoor eating.

Kath Donovan and her family liked barbecues so much that they even had them on special occasions.

For my Mum and Dad's fortieth **wedding anniversary** we gave them a big barbecue. It was just our family, because with their seven children, and their partners, and the children, that was plenty to fit into the house and garden. We got them out of the house for the day, and got everything ready in secret. We made a big sign that said 'Happy Fortieth Wedding Anniversary', and fixed it onto the garden fence. We got all the food ready, and made lots of salads and things. People brought lovely things in for pudding. It was a really nice time – everyone had a lot of fun, because we all enjoyed barbecues, and it was a lovely day too.

It was much better than a meal in a hotel, or something like that, because we could all wander around, and the kids could go off and play and didn't have to be good all the time.

School 1

In the 1980s, there were a lot more computers in primary schools. Children were taught how to use them when they were very young.

Joe Shuter learnt how to use the computer in his primary school.
In our school we used the computer a lot. We all wanted to use it, so our teacher made a **timetable**, to make sure that we all got a turn. It was fun. You could play games with numbers, or draw, or play games where you had to read instructions on the screen to get to the treasure. We also typed up our stories on it, sometimes. I really liked this, because my handwriting wasn't very neat!

Not everyone learnt to use school computers young. Henrietta Upcott had a teacher who didn't like computers.
We had a computer, it was a BBC – B, I think. Our teacher didn't like it. She had never used a computer in her life. She didn't know how to work it, and tried to pretend it wasn't there. We never used it for work, but because a boy in our class had one at home she let him show us how to play games on it at the end of the day.

Jane Gross was a teacher in the 1980s.

One nice thing about teaching at the time was that you could teach the things that you were interested in. You had to teach reading, writing, maths and some science, but after that you could teach what you liked, really. I liked history, so I taught my classes a lot of history. We did the Egyptians, the Romans and lots of work on castles, building and defending them. The kids really enjoyed it, and they learnt a lot.

Things like the castle building taught them a lot about things other than history, like technology and problem solving. We would often finish our work by doing something to show other classes what we had done. Sometimes we made a museum for them to visit, sometimes we decorated the entrance hall. Sometimes we did a play, like the children in the picture. Making all the costumes and working out the story taught us a lot about the Romans.

Children performing a play in the school hall. From the costumes you can tell that this play was about the Romans.

School 2

A school sports day. Some schools practised a lot before sports day. They marked out tracks, and had team races. Other schools just had fun.

Jane Gross went to a serious sports day.

At my son's first school they took sports day very seriously. It really mattered who won. Lots of children got upset, and some of the mums thought that this was silly. We thought that the most important thing was that the children should have fun. So when it came to the mums' race we all ran hard until the end, and then we crossed the finish line all holding hands in a row!

Lucian Forbes went to a school where sports day was fun.

We used to enjoy sports day. We used to have all sorts of silly races, like one where you had to dress up your class teacher in silly clothes as quickly as you could. We did sack races too, and potato and spoon races. Our parents came to watch, and no-one had to do anything. Everyone cheered and yelled a lot, and everyone had fun. I can only remember one or two times where kids got upset at losing.

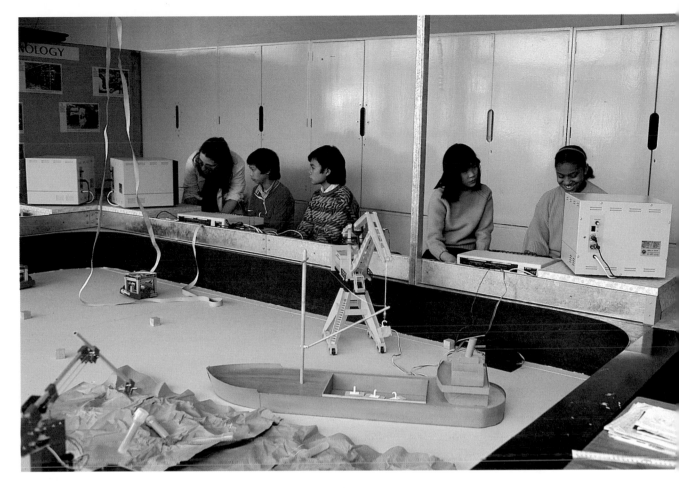

Older children did more difficult things with computers. These children are programming mini robots to move the way they want them to.

Caroline McCready programmed robots in her primary school.
There was a really good computer game where you had to tell the computer what to do to put fruit into a big shopping basket. It wasn't complicated really, but it did mean that you had to do quite a bit of maths to work it out. I'm sure if our teacher had given us the maths to do as work in our books we would have been bored. But we all wanted to play the shopping basket game. It was fun.

Joe Shuter had to work a machine called the Roamer.
There were buttons on the top that you used to tell it what to do. The Roamer moved around, and you could make it go from one place to another by telling it how to move forwards, backwards, left and right. It would remember more than one instruction at the same time, so you could do complicated routes. There was also a button to make it turn around, and you had to tell it how many degrees to turn.

Work 1

The cars here were made by robots. If factories used robots to do boring jobs they needed fewer humans to work in them.

James Hudson lost his job when his factory started to use robots.
I worked in a car factory in Oxford. My job was boring, putting the same bit on a car all the time. But at least I had a job. When **robot workers** were first made, and our owners were interested in using them we were worried that we would lose our jobs. The owners said that they would still need people to look after the machines, and to make sure that they were doing things right. But then, when the robot workers were put in we were told that some people would lose their jobs. The owners said that they did need people to look after the machines, but that they did not need as many. They had to make about half of us **redundant**. They gave us older ones some money to **retire** early. There was no other work around, and the jobs that were going went to younger men. I felt lost having no work to go to each day. I had to go on the **dole**, which I had never had to do before since I went to work at sixteen.

Farms, as well as factories, used more machines instead of people. This combine harvester cut the corn, shook off the grain, and put it in the trailer.

Tony Hudson drove a combine harvester.

It was a horrible job, having to drive the **combine harvester**. It was usually hot, and dusty. All the **chaff** got everywhere. It was noisy. The harvester made all sorts of noise. There was the noise of the engine, and then the noise of all the different bits of the machine working – they made a lot of noise even when you had them all oiled. The noise was so bad that you had to wear **headphones** over your ears, to protect them. This was a law. It was proved that if you didn't do this you could hurt your ears, and end up going deaf. But the headphones didn't stop all the noise. They just made it a bit less loud, and they made you feel very cut off. You felt like the only person in the world. There was someone with you driving the tractor and trailer, but they had headphones too, so it wasn't really company. Some people had radios in the headsets, so you could talk to each other. Our boss didn't do that.

Work 2

Not all farms used new machinery. Some farms still harvested the old way. This was either because they could not pay for new machines, or because they did not want them.

Alan Lovell ran a farm in Somerset which did not use the new machinery.

My neighbour bought himself one of the new combine harvesters. He was very proud of it. He told me how much money it saved him, because he did not need to pay as many men to work for him. He said it harvested really well. I wondered about getting one. I talked to the man who drove his combine, and he said it was noisy, and hot and it jolted him about a lot. He wasn't happy working with it. He also said that you were more likely to hurt the animals that were living in the field, the mice and the rabbits. I would have had to borrow money from the bank to buy one, they cost a lot. And then I would have had the worry of paying it back. So I decided it was silly to have that worry, and less happy workers just to have the machine. I harvested in the old way. Everyone worked hard together. I'm not sorry that I didn't buy a combine.

In the 1980s, computers were used far more in many places. The place where they were used the most was probably in offices.

Paul Shuter worked for a company which produced books.
When I started in the office there were two electric typewriters, and only one computer. The computer was in the Managing Director's office. Most of the secretaries were still using **manual** typewriters. All the printing and the setting out of the books was done by printers in **printing works**. The people who wrote our books sent us their work either typed or hand written, but always on paper. But then computers changed, and the office changed too. Much more work could be done on computers. The people who wrote for us could write their books on computer, and send us the computer disc by post. We made changes to the book on the computer disc, on our computers. Then we sent the computer disc to the printer. It made things a lot quicker and easier. Now almost everyone in the office has a computer, and many of the people who write our books do too.

Spare Time 1

Home computers got cheaper in the 1980s. Clive Sinclair made cheap game-playing ones. His ZXSpectrum is in the picture.

Judith Maguire and her father had very different ideas about how a home computer should be used.

We got one of the very first Sinclair home computers. I think it was the one before the Spectrum. We got my dad to get it for me and my brother for a joint present – Christmas, I think it was. We loved it. We thought that it was great. What we liked doing most was playing all the games on it. They look hopeless now, because computer games have really got so much better very quickly. If you look at games from the 1980s now you think how bad the **graphics** were, and how long the controls took to do what you wanted. But then it was wonderful. Dad, though, thought that we ought to have it to learn how to write **programs** for it. In those days there weren't any computers that were just for games, like the Megadrive of Nintendo today. He made us learn Basic, the **programming language** of our computer, and do work on it too.

Kate Upcott joined two exercise classes in the 1980s.

I decided that I really wasn't very fit. There was a lot of fuss on the TV about how unfit people were, because their jobs did not give them a lot of exercise. People walked a lot less too, because so many more people had cars. After one of these programmes I decided that they were right, that I really didn't get any exercise at all.

There were lots of different exercise classes near where we lived. You could go swimming, do aerobics, dancing, weightlifting – I think there were lots of others that I can't remember. I decided to go to ballet classes, because I did that as a little girl. They were very tiring, but I did feel fitter. Then I decided to go to another exercise class as well, on a Wednesday morning. After a week or two I pulled a muscle in my leg. So I decided to give that up. I carried on going to ballet. I think that gave you all over exercise, and that was what I needed.

In the 1980s a lot more people began to worry about their health. They worried about the food they ate and they tried to keep fit.

Spare Time 2

Bikes were now designed to do more complicated things. Some could do stunts, like the one in the picture.

Peter Hudson wanted a BMX bike.

I remember when bikes stopped being just bikes that you rode to school and only had a few gears. Then there were the BMX ones, and they could do so much more. I saw a programme on the TV where these kids were riding the bikes in a big hall somewhere, Birmingham, I think. They were going down a huge steep ramp, and then up again just as far on the other side. It looked impossible! Some of the really good ones could make the bikes turn in the middle of the air, or stop dead at the top of the ramp.

We couldn't afford a bike like that. Most of my mates couldn't either. I remember that we got **skateboards** instead, and tried to do stunts on them. We made courses with ramps to jump off, logs to get over and things like that. When we got good at the course we made it more difficult, or tried doing the whole course standing on our heads on the skateboards!

Video recorders were popular in the 1980s. At first there were blank tapes to record TV programmes. Then you could rent films. People felt this would kill the cinemas.

Jane Gross stopped going to the cinema in the 1980s.

We rented a video recorder in 1981, and had some friends round to watch a film we hired from the local rental place. It was dreadful, it must have been a bad copy, it was so dark that you could hardly see what was going on. But then we joined another rental club, and found that the films were as good as TV. To begin with we rented films *and* went to the cinema. But when we had our son, Joe, it was so much easier to hire a film than to arrange for a babysitter and go to the cinema. They also started leaving a shorter gap between things being on at the cinema and out on video. And renting got cheaper. We thought we'd never go to the cinema again! But it's not the same at home. You don't have the big screen, and the sound all around you, and the popcorn and the nice feel of a cinema. Now Joe is nine, we have started going to the cinema again, all together.

Spare Time 3

There were a lot of new sports that were popular in the 1980s. These people are windsurfing, also called sailboarding.

Sarah Warbrick learnt how to windsurf whilst on holiday in the South of France.
You actually start learning how to windsurf on dry land! The instructor showed us all the basics and it was about half an hour before we were allowed in the water. There were ten of us going out to sea at once. Each of us had a line attached so that we wouldn't get lost at sea. However, it was still very chaotic. We all kept bumping into each other and falling off our boards every few minutes.

After the first day, I really felt I'd got the hang of it. So off I went, without my safety line. It was very exciting, speeding across the water. Then I realised that I couldn't turn round. Luckily I was rescued by an experienced windsurfer. It was good fun though, everyone should try it.

There were lots of clubs for children. Some of them were after school, so that the children of working mums were looked after. Some were in the evening.

Alice Vickers went to an evening youth club when she was about ten years old.

The youth club ran from 8pm to 10pm. You could turn up when you felt like it, and go when you felt like it. You paid a pound for life membership, then 20p every time you went. There were lots of different things that you could do. There was snooker, like in the picture. That was quite fun, as long as you could find someone who was as good at it as you were, or as bad at it as you were! You could also play all sorts of outdoor games on the field. There was a room for watching TV or listening to music, and there was a shop that sold sweets, crisps and drinks. You could do painting, or join in quizzes. I think that there was table tennis too. I liked the snooker and the quizzes best. I like the snooker because my friend and me were just as bad, so we could get better together. I liked the quizzes because I was quite good at getting the answers right!

Holidays 1

In the 1970s and 1980s young people could buy a railway ticket and travel on European railways for a month. Once they bought the card they didn't have to pay to travel.

Jane Gross went on an InterRail holiday.

These holidays were called InterRail holidays. The rules were different in different years, but when we went you had to be under 26 years old. We were 25 when we went. We went with a friend of ours, and stayed in France, Italy, Yugoslavia, Hungary and Austria. When you bought the ticket you got a booklet, which the **conductors** on the trains had to stamp as you travelled. You had to make sure that you had all the right stamps in your passport that let you go into some countries, like Hungary. It was wonderful, and I think we would have gone again, but we were too old the next year. It was very tiring, because we tried to travel as cheaply and as far as possible. The best way to do that was to travel at night and sleep on the floors of trains. That way you didn't miss daytime in a place, you slept free, and you travelled at night.

Many people still went on day trips instead of holidays. You could go to the seaside, to adventure parks, or to places which showed you what life was like in the past.

Alice Vickers worked in Cogges farm, Witney, which showed what life was like on a farm in the early 1900s.

We used to visit Cogges a lot when I was very small. I loved going there. I got to know the people, and found out that they gave people jobs there. As soon as I could I got a job there. They wanted children as well as grown ups because in those days children started to work really young. I got a job in the kitchen. I had to wear a long brown skirt, a white blouse and apron and a frilly 'mop' cap. I also had to wear black lace-up boots. I worked in the kitchen. We worked all the time, really trying to work all day as if we were really living there, but stopping to answer questions if visitors asked them. When I started all I did was wash up and take scraps to the pigs or to the compost heap. Then I was allowed to collect fruit and peel the vegetables. Later I helped the cook, making pies and things.

Holidays 2

In the 1980s, a lot of people went on 'working' holidays. They did something that helped the environment. The people in this picture were making a drystone wall.

Peter Hudson went on one of these conservation holidays.

When I was a student I once spent the whole summer holiday on a **conservation** holiday. I answered an advert in one of the college magazines. The people paid you a very small amount of money, only two or three pounds a day for you to buy food, and they provided you with a place to stay. This place turned out to be a biggish house somewhere in the middle of the Yorkshire moors. There were two male and two female dormitories, with about ten beds in each. The people who were running the holiday slept on the next floor. The funiture was all very old and broken, and the cooker only partly worked. Also, there were so many dogs and cats in the house that it was full of fleas.

But the actual work was interesting. We learnt how to mend walls, to look after hedges to make sure that the wildlife in them was OK. It taught me a lot about looking after the land.

Jane Gross went to Disneyworld with her family.

We went to Disneyworld in December 1989. I remember because it was over our son's sixth birthday. He was very excited about going. I wasn't sure that I wanted to go. I thought it was going to be just a giant fun-fair, and I don't like fun-fairs. Most fun-fair rides make me feel sick. I wasn't really expecting to enjoy myself very much. Paul, my husband, had been to Disney in the 1970s, the other one, because they were staying with relations in San Francisco. He told me what it would be like, but I still wasn't ready for how big it was. It was huge. One ride, the Haunted House, had an actual house built there! The place was enormous, and the rides had been done so well, with lots of details. There were lots of rides that didn't jerk you about or make you feel sick. We went in the winter. In summer you had to queue a lot, up to half an hour for each ride. That would have spoilt the fun a bit.

A picture of Disneyworld, Florida. In the 1980s, flying across the Atlantic got a lot cheaper. People could afford to go to America.

Special Days 1

Bouncy Castles were very popular in the 1980s. People hired them for parties, and they were often used at fêtes or fairs.

Joe Shuter went on lots of bouncy castles.

When I first went on a bouncy castle, I was a bit scared. I was only four at the time. They made you take off your shoes and socks. That seemed really strange, and I remember wondering why I had to do that. I didn't know what to expect. There were lots of big kids on it, so I felt a bit confused, and tried to walk, not bounce. I wobbled all over the place, and kept falling over. I got the hang of it just as we were all told we had to get off, so my mum said I could have another go.

I've been on them at fêtes and I went to a party once where they had hired one. They are great fun. It is really noisy. The kids make a noise, and so does the machine that keeps blowing air into the bouncy castle the whole time. You have to really yell to be heard! If there are little ones on too, I try to remember what it was like when I was little, and I try not to crash into them!

Chester Kamen played his guitar on stage at the Live Aid concert.
I had played lots of different concerts, but never one as big as this, or with such an amazing feel to it. There was such a huge audience. It is difficult to describe how big the audience was, or how excited everyone was. You would have to have been there to understand how special it felt. I was playing guitar with Bryan Ferry. I really enjoyed it when I played a guitar **solo**, with everyone in that huge place listening.

My family watched, and afterwards they said that the TV cameras were on the wrong person for that bit, and they were yelling at the TV to show me! There was only one problem. The show was to raise money for the people in Africa, and backstage Bob Geldof, who organized the whole thing, was going round with a bucket, getting people to put lots of money in, as well as having come to play for free. I couldn't afford to give much, and I felt sad I couldn't give more.

The Live Aid concert in 1985. This was organized by the pop star Bob Geldof, to raise money to help people affected by famine in Africa.

Special Days 2

A party in a Wimpy Bar. In the 1980s people had their parties out more often. They hired a restaurant, or took the children swimming or ice skating.

Caroline McCready went to several parties at Sweeney Todd's Pizza Parlour.

Parties at Sweeney Todd's were really good. It was much better going out to a place like that than going to a party in the house of the birthday person. It seemed more grown up. The food was the sort that you liked to eat, and the parents were more relaxed about it all, too. We would all meet there, and there would be a special table for us. The tables were really long and were decorated with balloons and streamers. I think there were special party plates, but I can't remember that for sure. Then you chose your meal. You could have pizza, hamburger and chips or sausage and chips. The sausages were the biggest I have ever seen in my life, about 30 cm long! You also got a drink. The birthday person was given a free Sweeney Todd tee-shirt and a big special balloon. Some of the people who worked there, joined in and sang 'Happy Birthday to You'.

Glossary

ball pit a play area full of coloured plastic balls, usually about 1m deep. Children climb about in them. It is difficult, as the ball keeps moving about.

chaff the outside case on a piece of wheat or other grass crop.

combine harvester a machine which cuts the wheat, shakes off the chaff, collects the grain, and bundles up the stalks all in one machine.

conductors people in charge of collecting fares on public transport.

conservation wanting to save or look after the environment or some part of it.

dole unemployment money, paid to you by the government if you can't get a job.

famine famines are when lots of people are starving because they do not have enough food.

gadgets things which have been invented to do jobs around the house. A tin-opener could be called a gadget, so could an electric mixing machine.

graphics pictures.

guttering guttering goes around the edge of the roofs of houses to catch the rainwater and take it to the drains.

headphones a pair of small speakers or sound mufflers, one for each ear, mounted on a band.

manual by hand. Manual typewriters had no electric power to make typing easier. You had to hit the keys a lot harder.

power cut when the electricity stops working.

printing works the place where books, magazines and papers are printed out.

programming language the way that people get computers to do things.

programs commands to computers that make them do something.

redundant no longer needed. To be made redundant is to lose your job.

retire to stop working, by choice, because of your age. Men usually retire at 65, women at 60.

robot workers robots designed to do a simple job which was once done by people.

scramble nets rope nets, which can be 1m square to much bigger, which go up from the floor to somewhere higher up. The ropes make square holes about 30cm around. You use these to climb up.

skateboard a board with four wheels, about 1.5m long and 30cm wide. They are often decorated. They are curved up at each end. You balance on them and try to do complicated tricks.

solo a song or piece of music performed by one person.

timetable a list of times when people can use things or when people have to be in certain places. Timetables are also made for trains and buses.

utility room a room for the noisy kitchen machines, like the washing machine, the drying machine, and sometimes the dishwasher too.

wedding anniversary a celebration of the day you got married.

Index